FUGUE

AN AURAL HISTORY

✿

FUGUE

AN AURAL HISTORY

✦

JULIE MARIE WADE

NEW MICHIGAN PRESS

TUCSON, ARIZONA

NEW MICHIGAN PRESS

DEPT OF ENGLISH, P. O. BOX 210067

UNIVERSITY OF ARIZONA

TUCSON, AZ 85721-0067

<http://newmichiganpress.com>

Orders and queries to <nmp@thediagram.com>.

ISBN 978-1-934832-90-5. FIRST PRINTING.

Design by Ander Monson.

Cover image: photo 20907444 © Alexis Bélec | Dreamstime.com.

CONTENTS

For Angie Griffin,
music to my ears

❈

"A sound accomplishes nothing; without it life would not last out the instant." —*John Cage*

"Listen! Listen, and I will tell you how it happened." —*Edgar Allan Poe*

✿

I was born on a Sound. It was mostly quiet there. Sometimes a foghorn blared in the white smear, and we startled. The light was much more dangerous than the dark. This is often the case.

Ferry boats passed in the harbor, resisting collision. Arrived at the docks safe and sound. The front of those boats is also the back. They never turn around.

Our water was soft, salty, and cold. Recessed from an ocean we couldn't see. Overflow seating.

All day we watched a Sound from our windows. From a hill overlooking the Sound. My parents still live there. I only visit in dreams.

I liked the idea that a Sound could be seen. It tickled me. My own senses were always conjoined. Naturally, you could watch an aural event, listen to a visual occasion.

The Sound rippled, and we watched it. Sounds rippled, and we listened. The splash of my father skipping stones in the Sound.

The echoes of my father in me.

"Why is it called that anyway?" I asked.

"A stone?"

"No—a Sound."

"Because sailors were so happy to reach safe passage, they called the inlet Sound."

❊

In primary school, we were given recorders.

Did our parents pay for these? Were they ours to keep? And if so, where has mine gone to now?

I may have practiced once. The noise was not like music. My fingers covered some holes, then uncovered them. I cannot recall recitals, only drills in music class.

Where did we store them? How did we know which one was ours? Was there a box that buckled like a briefcase, flashes of plush red velvet inside?

I did not love my recorder. Could not. Would not. I did not wish to play. Ugly cousin of the flute. Overgrown whistle. What

I resented most was the promise that seemed reneged upon: A recorder is a device used to record something.

My father had one—black box with a clumsy plug. I hid it in the jade plant to record my parents' conversations. Cumbersome, hard to disguise. You had to depress the "play" and "record" {so audaciously red!} buttons at precisely the same time.

What I wanted was a small recorder, the kind detectives carried, with a tiny cassette tape inside. You could keep it in your pocket, tuck it in the glove box of your car. Slip it under a fern-frond. No one would be the wiser.

I played poorly on the recorder. *JMW lacks enthusiasm for this instrument.* Who could blame me? I wanted to *record* something. Two buttons at once: *Thwack!*

What I might have said if someone cared to ask: "The human voice is my favorite kind of music."

❋

aperture, bicuspid, cantilever, deleterious, enigma, fricative, grenadine, hallowed, intimations, julienne, kaleidoscope,

❋

As I practiced words aloud for the spelling bee, we idled in traffic. Onomatopoeia: *idle* is the sound the car makes at stoplights: tremble-hum, low vibration.

In spelling, I sometimes confused them: advice and advise. The "ice" that melted, the "eyes" that saw. But I knew I favored the "c" over the "s" because it was versatile—sometimes sibilant, sometimes cacophonous. The "c" had a soft and a hard side, too, like the woman I aspired to be.

❈

What are the sounds of your childhood? {prompt I give in class and write along with my students}: My father, unfolding the newspaper at the dinner table and smoothing it along its seams; my mother's electric typewriter, buzzing as she turned it on, then the fast-clack of the keys as she began her 70-words-per-minute firestorm; the smack of a croquet mallet when we played after summer dinners on the plush front lawn; banging pots and pans with wooden spoons at midnight on New Year's Eve; foghorns; crinkly parkas; the surprisingly harsh *thwump* of toe shoes as the older girls at the studio rose and spun, rose and spun, turning to cotton candy before our eyes; blowing into empty bottles I found on the beach; jumping on bubble wrap; tearing a page from a Mead spiral notebook—*spontaneous perforation!*; playing "Peter Peter Pumpkin Eater" on the shiny black keys of the old upright piano {the true extent of my musical interests and abilities}; hooking the inside of my cheek with my index finger and making a sound identical to the

Pringles can unpopping in television commercials {we weren't a Pringles family after all}; the vacuum cleaner lulling me to sleep with its gentle roar {*oxymoron!*}; my father's roll-top desk sliding shut; the silver clappers on my tap shoes as I shuffle-ball-changed to show tunes with my mother; dutifully, every night before bed, my father winding the grandfather clock; daily, my mother shouting, my mother screaming, my mother shrieking {gradations of rage}; daily, my father's low, steady voice trying to calm her; the windows slamming abruptly shut; the conch on the kitchen sill—how I pressed it hard to my ear till the ocean drowned out all the other sounds.

※

In primary school, some older students played in Bell Choir, and some older students played the chimes. There was no Chime Choir, not officially. Chimes were merely the province of those who aspired to play the bells but failed.

No one knew why.

Sometimes the Bell Choir played at school assemblies. Sometimes the Bell Choir did not. Sometimes chimes were played as precursor, like the dull prologue to a picaresque novel. Sometimes chimes were not played at all.

You have to understand the chimes were plain and gray and fit into your palm like relay sticks. Their clappers were visible on the outside. No mystery there.

Who designed such a hideous contraption? I slumped in my pew. *What reject from percussion school was responsible for this? Oh, how the chimes incensed me with their lack of elegance! This was a chime? The wind chimes on our back porch could do better.*

The teacher made me watch. Eyes forward, back straight. Music appreciation! I couldn't hear them because I could see them. The sight destroyed the sound.

But the bells!

The boys and girls wore gloves. White gloves. Like putting-on-your-stockings-before-church gloves. There were small, high-pitched bells and large, low-pitched bells. The table was long and covered with white cloth. Communion cloth. Like preparing-the-Lord's-Supper sacred cloth. On it, the bells were arranged by size and sound.

The smallest girls rang the smallest bells. The largest boys rang the largest bells. Our teachers so unoriginal in this regard. Boys with hairy forearms, boys whose voices had already begun to change.

It seemed you had to have acne and a patchy goatee if you ever hoped to ring a massive bell. I watched their muscles straining as they raised them—those lucky boys, those entitled boys! Not just a *ding* or a *dong*, but the robust reverberations of the heaviest bells.

One day I would do it! One day I would ring the biggest bells, the deepest bells! I would flex my arms and fling my wrists, and the listeners would be transformed!

I leaned forward in my pew, neck craning toward the next row. The teachers made me right myself. Eyes forward, back straight.

But the bells!

They had to practice after class, my parents said. They had to polish the handles and bodies of the bells. To care for them like a pet, like a child. What kind of commitment was I prepared to make?

I would give anything! I would give everything!

In the end, I left that school the same year my belligibility {portmanteau!} began.

Where did they store them? How could I find them?

The bells were mysterious, like the girls I loved—out of the question and just beyond reach. I never even touched one.

❊

My father always complained of water in his ears. In the summer, often, an infection called "swimmer's ear." He took to wearing plugs in the ocean and the pool. Sometimes, so as not to forget to put them in, he wore the plugs for hours. My mother or I would be calling to him, waving and clamoring, but he couldn't hear us at all. I assumed he moved through the world in blissful silence during those times—perhaps a silence he preferred.

But then, when I was grown and my own ear canal was blocked with wax, I discovered a symphony inside my body. Everything amplified: a swallow, a rumble, the iambic rhythms of my own heart. The world sounded the way it did under water, surfacing slowly after a dive. And I knew then John Cage was right. {How had I ever doubted?} There is no true silence, only the absence of certain sounds, or the palimpsest of one set of sounds written upon another.

❋

look-see, marmalade, nonce, oasis, pandemonium, quill, rapscallion, synesthesia, tacit, umbra, verisimilitude, wince,

Before I read the story in high school, I imagined "The Tell-Tale Heart" would contain quite a different narrative—someone trying to move on from love whose heart kept betraying them. It was hard to let go. I hadn't done it myself, and still I knew. {*Foreshadowing:*} One day I would leave my whole world and start again somewhere else.

So I didn't expect the madman, no. I didn't expect the murder. But I understood the guilt the madman felt, just as I recognized the heightened quality of my own senses when I began to plan my escape. "My sense of hearing especially became more powerful. I could hear sounds I had never heard before. I heard sounds from heaven; and I heard sounds from hell."

In one ear, I heard my mother chanting, "Don't waste water!" over the rush of shower water, her hand wiggling the door knob, then pounding on the wall. In the other ear, I heard my father speaking softly—*why did this seem more sinister somehow?*—"You must heed your mother's wishes in all things and trust that she knows better than you do."

A voice in my head was narrating a story, too. "What about what I want?" the voice whimpered. "Am I not allowed to have any privacy, any time and space alone?"

Our teacher Mrs. M. tapped my desk like a raven at the door. "You've been awfully quiet today. What strikes you about 'The Tell-Tale Heart'?"

I was slow to speak at first, cautious in my reply. "Well, it's a frightening story to read—because it's a killing story, and it's told from the perspective of the killer. But then after you read it over a couple of times, you start to wonder if it's even meant to be taken literally, you know?"

"Interesting." Mrs. M. liked me. I knew she did. Which meant she would grant me a certain freedom to meander toward my answer—nothing like the canned responses some of our nuns required. "So, what does this story mean to you *figuratively*?"

My palms left sweat-streaks on the desk, and the desk wobbled like a grocery cart. Finally, I said: "It just seems like we all give ourselves away in the end."

Some girls were snickering, but others fixed their eyes on me intently. I had a flicker in my head just then that I might like to be a teacher, then a second flicker of my mother wagging her finger, warning, "*Never* be a teacher. They can't pay you enough to make all the hassles worth it."

My cheeks were probably flushed, and by then I was probably speaking too fast, but I continued as Mrs. M. nodded along. "Like here, where the narrator says, 'My head hurt and there was a strange sound in my ears.' He tries to ignore it, but the sound is just a manifestation of his feelings. He's done something wrong, and he can lie to the police about it, but ultimately, he can't lie to himself. He might have even gotten away with his crime, but it's not the old man's heart he keeps hearing in his ears. It's his *own* heart that's tell-tale. And I think—or at least I think Poe thinks—that's how all our hearts are."

Mrs. M. was smiling at me in a prescient way, the way I would someday smile at my own students. I took a breath and let myself slowly exhale. Hearts were insistent, I realized. If we tried to ignore them, they would only grow "Louder, louder, louder!" And hearts didn't just pronounce guilt. Sometimes they also announced desire.

*

Go ahead, tell me—what words do you love? For to love a word is to love the sound it makes. To love a word is to hear the bells in it; to use a word out of love is to become a bell-ringer, which is also to say, a *campanologist*.

xylophone, yuletide, zephyr, anaphora, bereft, clemency, deckled, endow, foreshadowing, granular, harrowing,

❁

It was a library copy, tall, hard-bound and hot-pink with a sheer plastic cover. No picture on the book jacket, which only heightened the suspense. In large, cream letters, the title: *The Heart is a Lonely Hunter.* I had to let it sink in. A sentence for a title. Also a metaphor. Also a declaration. Below the title: *By Carson McCullers.*

I assumed Carson was a man, like Nancy Drew's father, police chief Carson Drew. At seventeen, assigned to read this book for AP American Literature, I sat on my bed and felt the volume vibrate. The look of the book {feminine and imposing at once!} and the feel of the book {those deckled pages!} and the smell of the book {an intoxicating must, like the reading itself!} all conspired to change my relationship with "course text," with "class assignment."

A woman had written this book. A woman had written and published this book when she was just six years older than I was then. A woman who married the same man twice. A woman who also loved women. A woman who only lived to be 50. A woman who heard music in every word.

The first sentence: "In the town there were two mutes, and they were always together."

Such simple language! I was not used to big books that spoke softly. I was not used to small words that spoke volumes.

One of the mutes was a man named Singer. How could he sing without speaking, I wondered? Was his name ironic, or was it more of a koan, like the Zen thought-riddles we studied in World Cultures class?

I made a note of this: *Silence might not mean the absence of song.*

There were other things, too. Singer and Antonapoulos lived together for 10 years. They did not speak, and they did not hear {I wasn't sure if *deaf-mute* was a pejorative term?}, but of course they saw and touched, smelled and tasted. Of course they tended rich, interior lives—though the book implied Singer's was richer. And they *felt*. They felt so deeply for each other.

"Was it just friendship?" I asked in class.

Another girl snapped: "What else would it be? They understood each other without the pressure of words."

I had never thought of words as pressure before. I had only thought of words as release.

When Antonapoulos was sick, Singer cared for him. When he became befuddled, unhinged, Singer cared for him. When his cousin committed Antonapoulos to an asylum, Singer grieved for the absence of his friend. I marveled at how much their story resembled romantic love.

All the characters confided in Singer, and Singer confided in Antonapoulos by writing him letters and visiting him at the group home. Wasn't that what lovers did—reserved their most private truths for each other? At school, I kept trying to ask the question in different ways, but nobody wanted to hear. They *could* hear, but they chose not to.

Singer was tall and thin and wore a certain cloak of mystery. No one really knew him, even though his presence was pivotal to everyone's life. I noticed how Singer reminded me of my piano teacher. Whenever I saw his name on the page, I instantly pictured Mr. V-L. Their first names were both John, but nobody called them that. Singer was tidy and fastidious, working all day engraving silver at a jewelry shop. His work required the scrupulous attention that Mr. V-L said the piano required.

Did John V-L have an Antonapoulos in his life? Was he heart-broken over a lost love? And was that why, long past his childhood, he still lived at home with his parents? Was this return to his first home a way of coping with loss—the way Singer went to live in a boarding house with the Kelly family rather than live alone?

My mother, once: "For all we know, since he never married or had children of his own, your piano teacher may simply have never left home."

Me, in response: "But if *I* never marry or have children of my own, does that mean I can never leave home?"

That's when I learned some silences are loud as airplanes taking off or trains pulling into a station. Some silences blare like foghorns in a harbor, warning the approaching ships to steer clear.

Faye Webster

✶

incumbent, jubilant, koan, luxurious, magnanimity, nimble, oblique, perforate, quiddity, relinquish, sibilance,

✶

When I was small, to cope with the loneliness, I invented a sister named Kellie. The spelling was different, but the name was the same as the last name of the family from the book: Kelly. It was the most feminine name I could think of and also the prettiest green. Mostly, I liked the sound of it, and sounds carried connotations the way wind carried sails.

I didn't know then that "Kelly" could be a boy's name. I only knew that "Mick" was assumed to be a boy's name—not a reversible raincoat of a name like "Alex" {Alexandra} or "Sam" {Samantha}. But soon I began to ponder how gender resembled a reversible raincoat, too. One day I might face the world like a Mick, but the next day, I might face the world like a Kellie {Kelly}. And vice versa. And vice versa again. If I reversed the raincoat often enough, I would lose track of which side was the default side.

I didn't know then that androgynous Mick Kelly was widely believed to be a version of Carson McCullers herself—a glimpse of the author as misfit teen. But if you listened closely to the pseudonym, you could hear it: "Mick Kelly" and "McCullers." The echo of each in the other.

I wouldn't have said it then—I couldn't yet articulate—the queerness I sensed in Mick and also in the tenor of McCullers's prose. Carson and Mick sounded like old-town sheriffs sharing a beat. I pictured them with round bellies straining against their vests, eating donuts and drinking Sanka from an office pot. Then, faster than Mary Poppins could snap her fingers, they became a young woman and a girl again, an author and her own creation. I watched them walk together down a dusty road in the Deep South where I had never been, in a part of the country where my own true love would be coming from. Five years ahead. The book was a premonition.

Mick loved music, and I loved music, but we meant something different by the word. She meant the sounds an instrument made, and I meant the words on the page.

About Mick—and perhaps also herself—McCullers wrote: "That was the realest part of the summer—her listening to this music on the radio and studying about it."

I read all summer. I arranged words on lined paper the way some people arranged notes on a staff. Mick played the piano in her mind. The Kelly family didn't have a piano, but that didn't stop her from composing. {*Composing*: the same word, the same verb, for placing letters on a page or letters on a scale.}

We had two pianos in our Northwest home—two pianos while Mick had none. I wished I could have given her one. How tirelessly she worked on her symphony, *This Thing I Want, I Know Not What.* How tirelessly I worked on my novel, *Something Lacking, Something Gained.*

Later, Mick had sex with a boy and felt nothing. Or: she had sex with a boy and did not discover the music in his body, the music in hers. Sex was not a symphony, she learned. I thought of that scene, years later—how strange and strained it was—when I first had sex with a man.

Unlike Mick, sex didn't just happen for me. I planned for it. I decided it was the thing I wanted. Classic paradox: something surrendered in order to gain something else. Innocence bartered for experience. But like Mick, I learned something still was lacking.

Our AP teacher was a young woman from Georgia who had earned a Master's degree at Emory. The phrase sounded so romantic to me. She wore men's white Oxford shirts, swiveled a fat diamond on her thin finger. {Reversible raincoat.} Ms. K. was married but kept her maiden name. {Reversible raincoat.} She didn't wear dresses but did wear tall shoes like women usually wore with dresses. {Reversible raincoat.} I heard the South in Ms. K.'s voice and assumed she had chosen this book because it reminded her of home.

Late in *The Heart is a Lonely Hunter*, Singer kills himself after he learns that Antonapoulos has died. I raised my hand in class. "This is a tragedy like *Romeo and Juliet*," I declared, the first work of literature we were assigned our freshmen year. "Singer couldn't bear to live without his beloved any more than Romeo could."

Was it the same girl, or a different girl, or a chorus of voices that replied: "Stop making everything weird!" {*Weird* as synonym, as euphemism, for *queer*.} There was laughter in the room, though nervous. No one belly-laughed, but some girls tittered through their teeth.

Mick described an "outer room" where we live for other people, the place where we are viewed but seldom seen. She also described an "inner room," where few are granted access, where we sometimes hide even from ourselves.

Once, in the high school hallway, I burst into tears. Not like a balloon, with its finite burst. More like a pipe that kept trickling after. I heaved and sobbed with abandon. Ms. K. was powerless to comfort me. There was such kind concern in her eyes, as she touched my shoulder asking, "What is it? What is it?" It was not like me to break down, to reveal vulnerability in such a visceral way. The inner room had flooded, and the outer room began to fill with standing water.

I earned an A in her class, red and delectable as the fruit with which it is often paired: *A, as in apple.* But I could never look Ms. K. in the eyes again. I was *A, as in ashamed.* She had seen my "true colors shining through," just like the song said, and the glimpse must have been terrifying.

Perhaps because Ms. K. did not want to embarrass me further, she never wrote her words down. Instead, shortly before graduation, as I was stuffing my bag, rushing to leave, she spoke quietly and sincerely from across the room: "In college, you will be free, and I hope you will feel empowered, to explore the homoerotic subtexts in a great deal of American literature."

❈

What are the sounds of your adolescence? {prompt I give in class and write along with my students}: A lot of static and sitcom theme songs; the tender scrape of eyelashes on my pillow as I butterfly-kissed the cotton; how my stomach rumbled so loudly during fourth-period Health Class that another girl was prompted to ask, "Mrs. B., could you explain what *borborygmus* is?"{But the joke was on her because borborygmus was the best example of onomatopoeia ever!}; the way my mother's chandelier shook and the dishes in her hutches clattered during earthquakes that were never "the Big One;" my first Walkman, given to me on my sixteenth birthday, a birthday the Walkman and I actually shared—oh, how satisfying that click as the mixed tape my neighbor made began to pour like syrup into my ears! Counting Crows. *August and Everything After.* Angsty acoustics and the lingering sting of an electric guitar; car alarms as perpetual soundtrack to the '90s—look at a car funny, and it began to wail; foghorns; the stomp of my mother's feet overhead as I showered in the downstairs bathroom; the final *Jeopardy!* countdown, which was always playing even when it wasn't; cracking my knuckles, my ankles, my neck; the whirring tires of a tape rewinding in a VCR; punching the thick squares on my first word processor; clearing my throat, the perpetual *ahem* in it; my footfalls on a long road, sloshing in puddles, squishing in mud, the pebbles I kicked up as I ran; the rusty squeak of a three-hole-punch; the swift pierce of a stapler; the first time I heard my own voice and realized I liked it, reading a poem by Auden aloud—I liked the sound of it, and soon I began to like what it had to say.

❋

O, diacopic Poe! Onomatopoetic Poe! Poe whose name is more than partway to Poem. ¾. The last quarter saved for mystery stories. Poet Poe! *Poe....m!*

✿

In college, I had to choose a Physical Education course. As I considered the offerings paired with the professors' names, only one combination compelled: *Self-defense.......Hacker.*

Once, Dr. Hacker asked me to lift her onto my back using a technique we had learned in class. I carried her that way around the gymnasium, our arms linked, her back pressing into my back, her sneakered feet in the air.

Later, I learned she was a lesbian. Later still, I learned that I was.

✿

tenacious, undulate, vellum, whimsy, xenia, yearn, zealot, alibi, berth, cunning, doggerel, ecstatic, fennel, gravitas,

PART III

John Cage once wrote: "can you hear (externals, tympani, labyrinths in whack)?" Years later, I wrote back: "Dear John Cage, my labyrinths are hopelessly out of whack!"

❉

Carole Maso once wrote: "I wish my hand might touch the fire between the letters of the alphabet."

I have touched that fire. It is actual and metaphorical. For the synesthete, always both at once. *Perceived together.*

That fire is the torch I carry, the spark of light attending every sound. It's the heat rising off the printed page like the blue flame on our old gas stove.

Once, while reading a paper and cooking at the same time, the words caught fire, and as I watched them burn, it seemed—how to say this?—*familiar.* It was my most vivid experience of déjà vu. But for me, every *déjà vu* is also *déjà entendu.*

That is: if I have already seen it, I have already heard it, too. The fire on the page, the words on the page, all *crackling*, onomatopoetically.

❄

Once upon a time, the poet Sharon Olds was much younger than she is now. As I was. As you were. Her first book was published at an age I have already passed.

When A. saw the author photo on the back of that book, she gasped. "Sharon Olds looks just like my mother!"

I hadn't met A.'s mother yet, but later that year, I did, and noted the resemblance. Then, I saw a picture of A.'s mother when she was the age of Sharon Olds on the back cover of her first book. The two women might have been twins!

Earlier that year, after I met A. but before I met her mother, I had a chance to hear Sharon Olds read in San Francisco, but I missed it. I was too smitten to leave town, even for a weekend. My friends brought me a signed copy of her book—not the first book—a later book. This one was called *The Gold Cell*.

When my father-in-law says "cell," I think he's saying "sale." This is perhaps our most benign misunderstanding.

It's strange to think, though necessary to acknowledge: the newer the book, the older the author.

Once upon a recent time, I met Sharon Olds at a reading in Delray Beach. She was beginning to live up to her name. When my mother-in-law says "different," I hear the "rent" in it—like something not owned, or something torn. I try not to dwell on this sound.

At the reading, my ear was so painfully blocked that it kept popping open and closed. The pressure mounted, as though half my head had been submerged in water. Perhaps this was prolepsis of a kind. Perhaps I flashed ahead to a future where I was old and struggling to hear.

My new book had been accepted by a publisher under the title *Hourglass*. I was writing about time, meditating on bodies and how they move through time. My publishers changed the title to *Just an Ordinary Woman Breathing*, the final line of a Sharon Olds's poem, a poem which is quoted inside.

I wish I had known about the title change the night I met Sharon Olds. I wish I could have heard her better.

I remember thinking: *Some experiences transcend sound.*

Oh, how deeply I leaned into her silver aura! Oh, how closely I followed her lips as she spoke!

Sometimes now, when I'm reading aloud from *Just an Ordinary Woman Breathing*, I marvel at what a difference a single word makes. For instance: What if the book had been called *Just an Ordinary Woman Listening?*

When I say "listen," my tongue slides around in my mouth, trying to find the "t." It becomes a hand groping for a light switch in the dark.

❈

hiccup, imminent, joist, kerfuffle, lithe, middling, nubile, opaque, penchant, quell, remnant, stultify, tremolo, uvula,

❈

The morning of our wedding, we wake on a deflated air mattress beside the space heater on a friend's apartment floor. Sweat-shirted. Jet-lagged. Snowflakes flutter outside the window.

I whisper, "Hey, what's that sound?"

Groggy, she says, "What are you talking about?"

"Just listen," trying to conceal my smile. A. tilts her head, concentrates deeply. I lean over and kiss her cheek. "Don't you hear it?"

"Hear what?"

"Those are wedding bells!"

Her epic eye-roll. My grin from ear to ear.

❁

And the prize for best neologism goes to…*E.A. Poe*…for his triumphant creation, tintinnabulation!

❁

Once, in Palm Beach, A. and I were driving. A joy ride. We passed a sign that read Broken Sound.

"Did you see that?" Not: "Did you hear that?" We circled back. *Broken Sound Realty. Broken Sound Office Park.*

In Florida, of course, water surrounds us. Was there a real Sound or just a hole in the ground—more curated landscapes, fountains burbling beside a five-story garage?

"Can you imagine living in Broken Sound?" *The condos. The golf club. The community center.* Every day waking inside a shatter.

It wouldn't bother me, to tell you the truth. Sometimes the broken sound is the sound of someone getting out.

❁

Somewhere, just now, in an over-beige business suite—a water cooler exhales into a triangular paper cup: *glug! glug! glug!*

Somewhere, just now, in a Florida winter—a child cannonballs into a swimming pool. That *kerplunk* is a sound that becomes a splattering: aural, then tactile. Water droplets freckle the forearms of the most distant chaperone.

Somewhere, just now, a reluctant palm tree joins the communal *susurrus*. Not *circus* like big tent. Not *cirrus* like clouds. Synonym for *susurration*. The bounty of our language. That peculiar crinkle-whisper christened with its own word-sound.

❋

verve, winsome, xylem, yodel, zenith, avuncular, bramble, cauliflower, dendrite, expulsion, franchise, gratuity, howdah,

❋

Once, A. and I lived in a pink house in Dania Beach—pink as a cat's tongue, pink as the numeral two. After three years, without any warning at all, the landlord painted the house orange. This wasn't exactly the reason we moved, but it wasn't *not* the reason we moved either.

In the beachside highrise, building color didn't matter much. Everyone came for the sea. {See it! Hear it! Smell it! A sensory reverie!} Look to the west—there's *Ocean Drive* {namesake}!

Look to the east—there's the ocean {"the thing itself and not the myth"—Adrienne Rich}!

As a child, if someone asked my last name, I always said, "Wade, like *wade in the water*." I was born on a Sound after all. Shouldn't my name be a water-word? Better still, a water-verb, an action?

In the beachside highrise, where we lived for five years, the fire alarm sometimes malfunctioned. "The sensor is too sensitive," Management reported. "We are working to resolve this issue." *But isn't a sensor's job to sense?*

When the summer rains came, not the light *pitter-patters* but the hard *gush-thwacks*, the alarm would blare—sometimes for hours. "Heavy rains appear to be triggering our alarm system via the rooftop module," Management reported. "We apologize for any inconvenience this may cause."

A. and the cats and I, pacing and yowling. Humans covering our ears. No noise-canceling headphones yet. Cats under the bed. Cats under the couch. Humans and cats on the balcony, neighbors with cats and dogs and rabbits and cockatiels on their balconies. No one has earmuffs—it's Florida! No one has balaclavas {oooh, good word!}—it's Florida! The alarm still blaring. The firetruck racing down Ocean Drive, rain drops pelting and pinging, the heavy swoosh of the tires passing over the flooded road. Alarm still blaring. Firetruck still blaring. Two competing sirens—no harmony. *Sound the alarm!* So literal, so loud.

Later, I remembered reading how there was a once a persistent fire alarm in John Cage's apartment building; it "beeped all night." No one could find any peace except Cage: "I remained in bed, listened carefully to its pattern, and worked it into my thoughts and dreams; and I slept very well." The same man could enjoy a baby crying at a concert, the co-mingling of sounds. He refused to parse the world into "music" and "not music." Or perhaps he would only parse the world into "noise" and "noise." Either way: no hierarchy. A sound is a sound is a sound.

I too want to let the various sounds of the world work their way into my thoughts and dreams. I want to teach myself to listen *feelingly*, which is to say *receptively*, without favoring this sound as "music," that sound as "noise." Yet how does one not prefer? {I prefer A. to all other humans, and she has misophonia!}

Now, again, we live in a pink house in Dania Beach—pink as a plastic flamingo, or pink as a real flamingo after gorging on shrimp; pink as the numerals 12 or 22 or 2000. The fire alarms weren't exactly the reason we moved, but they weren't *not* the reason we moved either.

Our new house is full of new sounds. I try not to judge or dread them: the peculiar whine of the air conditioner, the shuddering pipes as the washing machine spins awake, the single stair that creaks intermittently, when humans and felines are nowhere near. I try not to favor one sound over another, even when our neighbor lugs her garbage bins to the curb long before dawn on Mondays and Thursdays.

"It's just M. across the street," I mumble in my half-sleep. "Listen. Try to tune in, not out."

❋

Vladimir Nabokov once wrote: "While S is not the light blue of C, but a curious mixture of azure and mother-of-pearl." My "s" is silvery, icicled, while my "c" is yellow as a pat of butter.

No two synesthetes alike, and no two perceivers either: A. insists the beach bag is blue. I insist the beach bag is purple. Is there an objective "true color"? Even the label does not say, so we compromise and call it "periwinkle."

❋

Our first year in the beachside highrise, we were awakened one night by a strange sound. Was it a timer on the microwave? A defect in the fuse box? A low-battery alert from the smoke detector?

In the dark, we stumbled out of bed. Light from the distant casino streamed through our living room window. A. thought it was tacky, but I admired that neon guitar—a whole building fashioned in the shape of an instrument. Down the hall we wandered. Into the bathroom with its chilly tile. Not the back-up beep of a delivery truck. Not the reminder beep on my retro wristwatch. *What was that sound?*

Then, in the kitchen, we discovered the source and stood mesmerized at the threshold. By the soft glow of stove-light, we could see the cricket—*had I ever seen a cricket before?*—huge and green, clinging to the cupboard door. The cricket was singing. Its song sounded somehow mechanical. We didn't recognize it as a natural sound—*but what, then, is a natural sound?* Not an alarm but a song. Perhaps the cricket was calling out to other crickets: *Where are you, friends? Where are you?*

We lived 10 stories high. We kept our doors and windows closed. How had the cricket found us? How had the cricket traveled so far alone? Even the cats came and stood at our feet and listened. This was before, we think, our elder cat went deaf. Everyone could hear the music, a private concert just for us.

I didn't know what would become of the cricket. Had he entered through the vent? Would he leave the same way?

For a long time, we watched and listened, awed by the gentle movements of his legs, and then we returned to bed, still listening.

In the morning, the cricket was gone, as though we had dreamed him. It has been five years, and we still tell each other the story of the cricket and his loud, insistent song.

"Remember the cricket?" we say—as if we could forget.

Later, we looked for a poem we loved:

"The cricket doesn't wonder /if there's a heaven /or, if there is, if there's room for him […] If he can, he enters a house/ through the tiniest crack […] He sings slower and slower./ Then, nothing." —Mary Oliver.

One beloved cat died. The other stopped hearing. The cricket never returned.

We adopted a kitten. We moved to a new house. A pandemic caged us in.

Fear is a lullaby, just like love, we learned. Grief is a lullaby, just like love. Both cats nestle at our feet in the bed, never worrying if there is room for them.

Now, if I close my eyes and press my ear close to memory's grate, I can still hear the cricket singing. Was it a blessing? Was it a warning? Perhaps it was a spell.

I try to conjure the bright green cricket in the solitary night. I try to remember the music a lone body can make.

✱

Do you keep your eyes *peeled* like potatoes or *pealed* like bells?

❋

We have entered the Zoom Era. Ironic name for going nowhere fast. I think of Mary Poppins hopping into sidewalk chalk drawings—analog, perhaps, to a screen. She "pops" in and out of places, just like her name. *Onomatopoetically.* Now I do the same, popping into Zoom rooms, "connecting to audio" as the dots dot and the swirl swirls. *You're muted!* we call loudly in unison—another irony. <u>*Unmute yourself!*</u> becomes our new refrain.

❋

intermittent, jugular, kumquat, linden, muumuu, noodle,
ontological, pompous, quandary, rhombus, sonic, taffeta,

❋

Somewhere, just now, on a quiet beach or a crowded beach, the ocean laps at the shore as a cat laps from a bowl. Soon, the same ocean will crash like silverware spilling from kitchen drawers. Soon, the same ocean will thump on the sand like a steady drum {*pa-rum-pum-pum-pum!*}.

Somewhere, just now, in a state park or a public garden—even in our own backyard—long stalks of bamboo are squeaking.

The wind moves gingerly among them, reed by reed, but they squeak together as ensemble, like strands of clean wet hair.

Somewhere, just now, perhaps on a campus where students have ceased to gather—a long black snake travels swiftly across a footpath. The sound of her smooth belly on the paved ground is nothing like a *slither*. Not a *skidding* either, for she retains full control. Not a *rippling*, or a *slicing*. No word has yet been coined to convey her locomotion through the grass, over the pavement, and into the grass again. Hear her appear. Hear her vanish.

❅

Outside our pink house, the Ron's Lawn Care truck ambles, backs into the curve of the cul-de-sac, with the slow, amplified beep of an aural ellipsis. I watch the dots of sound punctuate the sky from my office window.

On Zoom, my students can hear the weed whacker, the leaf blower, the lawn mower. Though the windows are closed, these sounds seep through—persistent, triumphant. I try not to resent them. I try not to view them as intrusions.

"Is there a way you can write these sounds into your work?" I ask the class. "Projective verse poets believed if a school bus passes your window while you're writing, then that school bus belongs in your poem."

"But doesn't that make the art less purposeful?" R. asks. "You always tell us how writers make choices."

Zoom informs me *my internet connection is unstable.* I jot the message down.

"We can choose to allow more of the world into our work. We can decide not to dismiss what may seem arbitrary as irrelevant."

Outside, a spinning blade catches a stone that ricochets off the stucco. A grinding sound, followed by a *schwing*, followed by a thud. Blue jays nesting in the plumeria tree voice a raucous revolt. Bird-song becomes bird-scold.

For many years, I said I couldn't teach remotely, digitally, online—so many ways of saying "apart from." Yet here we are, still together. Cyber-space is a space after all. It may not be the space I wanted, but it is, alas, the cherished space I have.

❀

Near the end of her life, the poet Mary Oliver moved to Hobe Sound. After her death, A. and I drove there to pay homage. It wasn't too far. We walked the shoreline, hard shells beneath our feet, a steady crunching. Height of summer, skin aflame, we finally plunged into the water. Then, her words floated as our bodies floated: "I only want to be a song."

❋

Today the candle burning on my office sill triggers the smoke detector. Alarms are alarming! Collective startle. My students see my full torso as I rise to swat the large white disk above the door. Collared shirt for the camera, sweat pants for the comfort, slippers since I'm not going anywhere.

Later, this moment will appear in student free-writes. A ruptured expectation. "We know but still forget," C. writes. "Our teachers are human, just like us. They can't control everything."

❋

For two years, I went nearly unhearing in the right side of my head. A clog that could not be cleared, even with the Debrox drops from the drugstore and the soft rubber ball syringe. I even learned a new word—*lavage*—meaning irrigation or flushing of the ear canals. *It's onomatopoetic, no?* The water *lavages* through the ear. First, the paradox of the slow rush, followed by a bubbling like seltzer, then a gentle, dissipating fizz.

The general practitioner sends in a nurse. She can see with her otoscope that I cannot hear. Then comes the relentless lavage—pressure building and building inside my head. But instead of release, there is blood. Not a nose-bleed—an ear-bleed. I watch her face contort. How I wish to console her!

I picture Mr. Gower, the heartbroken druggist from *It's a Wonderful Life*, boxing young George Bailey's ears. He's crying, and my child-self is crying, too. Pain is always a hot potato. It can even be passed through a screen.

"You're hurting my sore ear!" George wails. The film is black-and-white. The blood is likely chocolate syrup.

The nurse kneels, meets my eyes, apologizes. "I didn't mean to hurt you."

"It doesn't hurt," I say, surprised.

In the end, warm water trickles out, but the blockage never clears.

❊

Don't tell the young lovers. They are not ready to know they will not get to choose which parts of their lovers' bodies to love, how some touch may be loving and generous but not erotic at all. How A. will tip my head and let the cold drops fall into the labyrinth, then hold cotton to my ear and turn my face in her lap while the solution softens the wax. *10 minutes, 15, 20.* Such tenderness! I picture the mouths of clams buried beneath the sand, their breath burbling upward, pocking the otherwise-smooth. *The course of true love never did.* How she will steady me over our kitchen sink, use the dish-sprayer for improvised lavage. But despite her best efforts, no release.

"We could try candling," I propose. Not all proposals, even the candle-lit ones, are romantic. I nod to two hollow beeswax tapers and a printed guide.

"Do you want to rupture your ear drum? Should I just stick a Zippo in there and start sparking the ossicles, see if that does any good?"

I love her lexicon. {*Ossicles*, returning now—a long-ago spelling bee word!} I love also her quick wit and sharp tongue.

Of course love will not always see eye to eye, nor will love always hear ear to ear. "Well, candling worked for D.'s brother-in-law," I protest.

Decisive now: "No more DIY. You need to see an ENT."

❋

It's February in Fauntleroy, the tiny corner of Seattle where I came of age. Bright skies—"blue as cornflowers," the way the grandfather I never knew would say. He moved his family from Montana to this water-view inlet in 1953. On clear days, it's a mountain-view inlet, too. His wife outlived him by 36 years. Their house was sold this year to people I'll never meet.

When I lived here, this was a place that time forgot—*a whole landscape in fugue-state. It's always mid-century in Fauntlee Hills!* Anechoic chamber, like the inside of a snow globe, though our snow was mostly rain. We were isolated during those years. We "kept to ourselves." Reflections from the outside world—even the bustling city fifteen minutes away—were always held at bay.

Even then, I suppose, I was familiar with quarantine.

But the place I come from is trending now. Lines for the ferries have never been longer. We board on foot, my long-time partner, which is to say my brand-new spouse, and I. Married three days ago in Bellingham, we're venturing out into Puget Sound. No destination in mind, just "island-hopping."

Surely someone snapped a picture of us on the upper deck. Surely I have it somewhere. The water slaps the side of the boat as it dawdles in the harbor, but soon the ferry is moving. Then, it slices the water like a serrated blade. We are moving faster than I ever realized when I watched these boats from our kitchen window.

Most passengers are gazing toward Vashon as the ferry rushes toward the dock. But I am looking back toward Fauntleroy, a small pair of binoculars in my hands. There it is—not a beacon exactly, just a brick house with a red fence and a weathervane. Once home to me but now my home no longer.

I keep wondering if one of my parents will step out onto the deck, shading their eyes from the late winter sun. But even if they are watching, they will not see me. This has been true for some time. It wouldn't matter if I waved or called their names. And besides, certain squalls have quieted now. Today it's a kissing wind, not a biting wind. I stand aloft and wind-smitten, with no stones to cast. I trust A. and I will arrive on the other side, safe and sound.

❁

What are the sounds of your life right now? {prompt I give in class and write along with my students}: *PBS News Hour* played at low volume, Judy Woodruff's soothing voice as she recounts the world's horrors; air hissing from a punctured tire; the drip-drip of the bathroom faucet that catches my ear in the dark and holds my attention for hours; our sweet Tina pouncing on the printer as it springs to life, spitting out the pages and then dragging them back for double-sided ink; little slivers of the South in A.'s voice, just before she falls asleep; our sweet Tina pouncing on the bookshelf, volumes of poetry crashing and sliding across the floor; Javier, the postman, opening the mailbox with its signature creak, then pushing down the bright red flag; motorcycles whizzing past on the other side of the garden wall; squirrels chattering in the banyan tree; the hard thump of my gloves making contact with the heavy bag—punching, punching, punching, until my muscles quiver with relieved fatigue; our sweet Tybee softly snoring in a patch of catio sun; the loud white bird taunting Tina from the hedges, and Tina leaping, catching her claws in the screen; a delivery truck backing up; a garbage truck backing up; garage doors gliding open and shut at intervals; the chime of a new digital message; the distant thunder of a train; faintly, the ocean tossing itself onto the shore; and twice a week, in the evenings, as I drag the green trash bins down the drive, frogs everywhere emerging in the darkness, leaping joyfully in the grass, their huge eyes regarding me by porch-light—it isn't *croaking*, the sounds they make, but a euphoric and harmonized song.

✿

ubiquitous, virga, warble, xenogenesis, yowl, zaftig, abecedarian,
burnish, canticle, dwindle, esoteric, fumble, glow,

✿

One day I will teach Poe's "The Tell-Tale Heart" to college students in a Cultures of America class. I will share one of my favorite words—*epizeuxis*—the Greek word for an emphatic repetition of a single word or phrase over and over in rapid succession. *Louder, louder, louder!* Epizeuxis is meant to convey intense emotion.

One day I will travel with my beloved to the Poe Museum in Richmond, Virginia. One day I will travel with my beloved to the Poe Museum in Baltimore, Maryland. There are other Poe monuments we have yet to visit, a kind of Poetic epizeuxis to the writer himself—man of mystery, of many genres, of pervasive insight into what makes us humans tick.

One day we will stand together beside his tombstone during a light drizzle, sun obscured by clouds. Originally buried in an unmarked grave, we recognize the victory in this re-marking. Poe's own words became his epitaph: *Quoth the Raven. 'Nevermore.'*

When A. asks me how I would want my tombstone to read, I am only half-quipping when I say: *Quoth the Heart: 'More. More. More.'*

✳

The ENT, or more precisely the otolaryngologist, is Dr. Morse. *What would his code name be?* I chuckle to myself. He practices close to where I live and has hundreds of web-stars attached to his name. But his picture is what seals the deal: he resembles John Cage in vibrant old age.

Outside the hospital: a summer rain shower. I slip in the parking lot, the soles of my Toms not scuffed enough for good traction. Months now of sheltering-in-place, of not wearing shoes.

I follow the green arrows to a distant wing. I see no one the whole way there. My pink mask has llamas on it and covers my nose, mouth, cheeks, and chin with many folds of presumed extra protection. One ear hears everything; the other is so deeply plugged I am perpetually off-balance. My head aches, and my stomach flips. My heart thuds, unrelenting in my temples: *pow! pow! pow!*

"So, it seems you have some rather intractable wax," Dr. Morse begins as he enters the room. Even behind his mask, I can tell he is smiling. I nod. "Well, the good news is, I have a machine to take care of that."

As Dr. Morse inspects my ears, I realize I never thought much about my ears until I had trouble hearing. I'm sure this is a story he has heard before.

"There's a composer I like—well, he didn't necessarily appreciate that word—but he made music anyway, and he always referred to the ears as *labyrinths*. Does that seem fitting to you?"

Dr. Morse puts down the otoscope and begins a soothing lavage. For this, I sit upright, and he squirts warm water into my ears with something resembling a soap dispenser. No craning my neck or leaning to the side over a bucket.

When he finishes, he says, "Well, the ears are a-*maze*-ing!" To my delight, he mimes striking a drum and cymbals, adding the symbolic sound effects.

"Is it fair for me to ask—of ears, nose, and throat—which one is your favorite?"

Dr. Morse readies the machine. "First, let me ask *you* something: What do you for a living?"

"I'm a professor," I say. "I teach writing."

"Hmmm. What kind of writing?"

"Poetry, memoir, lyric essay," and then to clarify—"*creative* writing. Sometimes hybrid forms."

"Well, is one of those *your* favorite?"

I'm smiling now, too, and I wonder if he can tell from my eyes or from the sound my lips make splitting apart. "I guess I would say my favorite is whichever genre I'm teaching that day."

Dr. Morse inserts a tube into my troubled ear. In a matter of seconds, he has finished suctioning, and I feel a cool rush of air, a sonic lucidity. "Right now," he tells me, "the ears are my favorite."

The doctor's voice has become musical, every syllable sharp and clear. Already my head is lightening, my muscles loosening. "That's it?"

"*Bada-bing! Bada-boom!*" He stands in the safe-distance doorway and waves his gloved hand. "That's it."

✾

hectic, interlude, jargon, keen, loofa, mimeograph, nincompoop,
octagon, pom-pom, quorum, rescind, swimmingly, taut

ACKNOWLEDGMENTS

This book is a fugue of one sort (musical) but not another (amnesiac). In fact, it is the opposite of a fugue in that I am committed to remembering everything I can, which writing helps me do. And so this book belongs to you, my unforgettables: Annette Allen *in memoriam*, Dana Anderson, Bruce Beasley, Cate Fosl, Tom Campbell, Cindy Chinelly, Debra Dean, John Dufresne, Denise Duhamel, James Allen Hall, Brenda Miller, "The Outlaws" (Kim, Matt, Evie, Nolan "Super Hondo," and Sam Striegel), Suzanne Paola, Anna Rhodes, and my colleagues, friends, and students at Florida International University, in perpetuity.

I am grateful to John Cage for relentless inspiration, aleatory and otherwise.

I am grateful to Ander Monson and *DIAGRAM* / New Michigan Press for including this project in their chapbook series and for guiding it to print.

I am grateful to Angie Griffin, for these more-than-20-years and this more-than-I-can-ever-say.

Born in Seattle in 1979, JULIE MARIE WADE completed a Master of Arts in English at Western Washington University, a Master of Fine Arts in Poetry at the University of Pittsburgh, and a PhD in Interdisciplinary Humanities with a creative nonfiction dissertation at the University of Louisville. She has published an assortment of collections of poetry, prose, and hybrid forms, most recently *Skirted: Poems* (The Word Works, 2021) and *Just an Ordinary Woman Breathing* (The Ohio State University Press, 2020). With Denise Duhamel, she wrote *The Unrhymables: Collaborations in Prose* (Noctuary Press, 2019) and with Brenda Miller, *Telephone: Essays in Two Voices* (Cleveland State University Press, 2021, selected by Hanif Abdurraqib as the winner of the Cleveland State University Press Nonfiction Book Award. A winner of the Marie Alexander Poetry Series and the Lambda Literary Award for Lesbian Memoir, Wade teaches in the creative writing program at Florida International University in Miami.

❋

COLOPHON

Text is set in a digital version of Jenson, designed by Robert Slimbach in 1996, and based on the work of punchcutter, printer, and publisher Nicolas Jenson. The titles here are also in Jenson.

❀

NEW MICHIGAN PRESS, based in Tucson, Arizona, prints poetry and prose chapbooks, especially work that transcends traditional genre. Together with DIAGRAM, NMP sponsors a yearly chapbook competition.

DIAGRAM, a journal of text, art, and schematic, is published bimonthly at THEDIAGRAM.COM. Periodic print anthologies are available from the New Michigan Press at NEWMICHIGANPRESS. COM.